FROM TIP TO TAIL

The Layman's Guide to Basic Alpine Ski Tuning

By David J. Rader

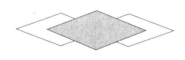

Illustrated by John F. Boyd

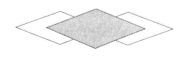

Cornerstone Publishing Company
Wichita, Kansas

From Tip To Tail:
The Layman's Guide to Basic Alpine Ski Tuning
By David J. Rader

Copyright © 1994
Second Edition © 1995
Cornerstone Publishing Company
10803 E. 21st Street
Wichita, Ks. 67206

Printed in the U.S.A.

ISBN 0-9645550-1-8

To Dad—Your tree still grows...

❄ TABLE OF CONTENTS ❄

Sturdy support of the ski is a must if you want to do the job right!

> ❄ The Ski Vice
> ❄ The All-Purpose Bench Vice
> ❄ Retracting Ski Brakes

1. Base Cleaning
A clean base is an essential start to any ski tune.

> ❄ Solvents & Other Cleaning Agents
> ❄ Evaporation Time

2. Truing the Base
A ski base may become either concave or convex through wear and tear. You will learn to flatten the base to ensure optimum control of the skis.

> ❄ Base Contour Conditions— Flat, Concave, Convex
> ❄ Treatment of Convex Base
> ❄ Treatment of Concave Base

3. Filling in the Gouges

You will learn how to melt P-tex (base material) into gouges in the base of your ski, then scraping off the excess to make it flush with the base.

❋ Gouge Contamination
❋ Application of P-tex
❋ Removal of P-tex

1. Flat-Filing the Edge

You will utilize mill bastard files, or special edge sharpening tools to "improve your edge."

❋ Sharpening Bottom Edges
❋ Sharpening Side Edges
❋ De-Burring Edges
❋ De-Tuning

2. Beveling the Edges

Beveling brings the edge up and off the surface of the snow, allowing for smoother glide and less chance of catching an edge in the snow. In most conditions, beveling is a recommended alternative to simply flat-filing your skis.

❋ Beveling Bottom Edges
❋ Beveling Side Edges

A slightly textured ski base has been proven to glide faster than one that is smooth and glossy. Structuring the base is simply applying that texture.

❋ Methods of Structuring
❋ Trying New Patterns of Structuring

Waxing is the essential final step to any basic ski tune-up. You can't ski home without it!

❋ Applying Wax
❋ Removing Wax
❋ Post-wax Structuring

❊ INTRODUCTION ❊

In today's economy, we all agree that it is both wise and necessary to save money at every opportunity. This is especially true given the rising costs of our recreational activities.

You have joined the ranks of do-it-yourselfers who are discovering that tuning your skis at home can not only be a tremendous way to save your hard-earned money, but also one of the most gratifying hobbies that you will ever undertake. By applying the principles of this fundamental instructional booklet, you will learn the art of ski tuning as performed by today's professional ski technicians.

Now you can achieve a fine ski tune in your own home and on your own time to ensure that your valuable investment not only lasts longer, but remains in peak performance condition. Best of all, your days of paying exorbitant prices for ski tunes are over!

The purpose of a ski tune is to maximize the performance potential of a ski. Like a musical instrument, a ski is capable of a certain level of performance, but without proper tuning it will never meet up to its full potential. It doesn't take an expert to notice the difference between a well-tuned set of skis and a set that has obviously been neglected.

So why tune your own skis? One reason, as already mentioned, is obvious—to save money. Certainly, you make an initial investment for the tools and supplies required for tuning, but it doesn't take long before you have completely paid for these by doing it yourself.

Another reason is convenience. You are able to tune your skis when you want, how often you want and where you want. Once you learn to tune skis, you have achieved independence and are no longer subject to someone else's time table or location. And finally, you will experience the satisfaction of a custom job well done—especially after that first run down the hill.

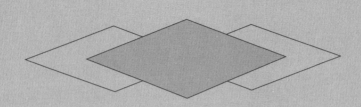

SAFETY TIPS

❋ Do not bend files when tuning, as they may shatter and become a safety hazard.

❋ Always work in a well-ventilated area whenever using solvents of any kind.

❋ Keep flames and extreme heat away from solvents or solvent fumes.

❋ Ski edges, scrapers, knives and cutting tools of any kind can be extremely sharp, so use caution whenever working near them.

❋ When burning P-tex (base material) use extreme caution! This material can become as hot as the flame itself.

❋ Always rely on the services of a certified binding technician to double check your binding retention settings and all other mechanical parts of the boot/binding system. A properly functioning system is essential to your own safety as well as the safety of those skiing around you.

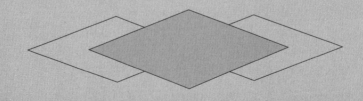

You have, no doubt, heard the phrase, "practice makes perfect." Nowhere is that more true than in the art of ski tuning. However, when tuning skis, it is also essential to use the proper tools to ensure a top-quality ski tune.

Take note of this list of basic tools and supplies that you will need in order to hand-tune your skis. Other optional tools and supplies are introduced throughout each section. Some may be purchased through a hardware store, but other, more specialized, tools can only be purchased at a ski shop. Most ski shops even carry handy tuning kits that supply most of the basic tools you will need for hand-tuning.

Remember that high quality tools can mean the difference between a good tune-up and an excellent one—and ultimately in the long life and performance of your skis.

Cleaning Solvents

Description, Use and Cost — For cleaning the base of a ski, use a gentle cleaner such as mineral spirits, or inexpensive isopropyl (rubbing) alcohol. These evaporate quickly and leave little residue behind. If you have a build-up of old ski wax left on the base, use a specialized wax remover, which is usually available in 6 to 10-ounce spray cans, costing about $5.00 to $6.00 each. Read all instructions and warnings on the container before using.

Metal Scraper Blade

Description, Use and Cost — The metal scraper blade is a flat sheet of steel about the size and shape of an index card. Use the metal scraper blade to scrape a ski base flat, or to remove the excess cooled P-tex (base material used for repairing the base) that remains after filling gouges in the base. Do not use a scraper for cleaning the ski base, as it may only permanently embed dirt and debris into the porous base material. The metal scraper blade can be purchased through a ski shop or hardware store for about $5.00 to $6.00.

Plastic Scraper

Description, Use and Cost — The plastic scraper is much the same size and shape as the metal scraper, but thicker. Use the plastic scraper during the waxing process to remove excess surface wax from the base of the ski. Again, do not use a scraper for cleaning the ski base, as it may drive dirt and debris into the porous base material. The plastic scraper can be purchased through a ski shop for about $3.00 to $4.00.

File Card

Description, Use and Cost — A file card is a stiff, metal-bristle brush used for cleaning out the debris from between the teeth of a file. The file card can be purchased through a ski shop or hardware store for about $5.00.

Wire Brush Face

Handle

Mill Bastard File

Description, Use and Cost — The mill bastard file is basically a flat metal bar with small blades milled into the surface. One end is usually square, while the other is tanged, or pointed. Use a mill bastard file to sharpen and bevel the steel edges of a ski—the 12-inch or 10-inch mill bastard file for initial filing, and the 8-inch file for more delicate, final filing work. The mill bastard file file can be purchased through a ski shop or hardware store for about $5.00 to $20.00, depending on the size, quality and brand.

Tang

Pansar Blade

Description, Use and Cost — A pansar blade, or pansar file, is similar to a mill bastard file, but the blades are much larger and curved for more aggressive cutting. Use the pansar blade to remove excess P-tex left on the base after repair, and to flatten a ski base that is in a convex condition. The pansar blade can be purchased through a ski shop or hardware store for about $10.00 to $30.00, depending on the size, quality and brand.

True Bar

Description, Use and Cost — A true bar is a straight metal bar, about 3 to 4 inches long and 1/2-inch in diameter. Some may be cylinder shaped, while others may be rectangular. Use it to judge trueness (flatness) of the ski base and the angle of bevel on the edge. These can be purchased through a ski shop for about $5.00.

Brass-Bristle Brush

Description, Use and Cost — The brass-bristle brush is a hand brush equipped with stiff, brass bristles for cleaning debris from the grooves in a structured base and directing any loose fibers toward the tail of the ski. You can purchase the brass-bristle brush at a ski shop. Prices range from $10.00 to $20.00 depending on the brand and model of brush.

Riller Bar

Description, Use and Cost — The riller bar, or rilling tool, is shaped much like a mill bastard file, but with small, sharp teeth specifically designed for cutting a grooved pattern into the base of the ski–the process known as "Structuring." The riller bar provides the cleanest structure of all. This specialized tool can only be obtained through a ski shop. It retails for $15.00 to $25.00, depending on the size and brand.

Surform® Tool

Description, Use and Cost — A Surform® blade looks somewhat like a cheese grater. These blades are replaceable and are formed to fit onto a Surform® handle, which can be pocket size, or a full 10-inch to 12-inch length. Use the Surform® to remove the bulk of cooled P-tex material left above the surface of the base after gouge filling. These can be purchased at any hardware store and cost about $8.00. Refill blades cost about $4.00.

Fine Whet Stone

Description, Use and Cost — The whet stone is a small, fine-ground stone block used to deburr the edges of skis after sharpening. These can be purchased in any ski shop or hardware store and sell for $5.00 to $10.00, depending on size, brand and model.

P-tex Candles

Description, Use and Cost — P-tex candles are small, round sticks—about 3/8-inch in diameter and eight to nine inches long. These clear or black polyethylene sticks, made roughly of the same material as the ski base, are melted and dripped into gouges on the ski base. Be sure to choose the proper color to match your ski base. These may be purchased only through your local ski shop and retail for about .75¢ each.

Ski Wax

Description, Use and Cost — Ski wax normally comes in a rectangular block, small enough to fit in your hand. A universal temperature wax will perform well in most conditions. Blocks of wax can be purchased at your local ski shop and cost between $3.00 and $6.00 each, depending on size, brand and temperature rating.

Scouring Pads

Description, Use and Cost — Scouring pads are rough, plastic fiber scrubbing pads used for fine structuring and buffing the base after waxing, or for cleaning the base in the preparation stage when grit and grime are caked on. Once you have used the scouring pad for cleaning, do not use it for buffing wax. You can purchase a package of two or three at most hardware or grocery stores for about $2.00.

Waxing Iron

Description, Use and Cost — The waxing iron can be any household fabric iron, preferably one without steam holes in the surface. Use the waxing iron to melt and drip ski wax onto the base of a ski and then to iron it into the porous base material. You can purchase a used fabric iron at thrift shops for about $10.00. Specialized waxing irons can be purchased at your local ski shop for about $30.00.

NOTE: **Refer to Appendix A for instructions on care and maintenance of tools.**

TUNER'S TIP NO. 1

"What's in a Name?"

Always tune your skis From Tip to Tail. If a ski is tuned from the tail to the tip, tiny burrs and shavings on the base are left protruding forward. This only creates drag on the skis.

Cost Estimate of Tools and Supplies

$ _____ Bench Vice or Ski Vice
$ _____ Cleaning Solvents
$ _____ Metal Scraper Blade
$ _____ Plastic Scraper
$ _____ File Card
$ _____ Mill Bastard File
$ _____ Pansar Blade
$ _____ True Bar
$ _____ Brass-Bristle Brush
$ _____ Riller Bar
$ _____ Surform® Tool
$ _____ P-tex Candles
$ _____ Ski Wax
$ _____ Scouring Pads
$ _____ Waxing Iron

Total $ _____

Attempting to tune a ski without the aid of a solid securing device is like trying to whittle a block of wood with one hand tied behind your back. Sturdy support is a must if you want to do the job right!

The Ski Vice

The sturdiest and most efficient tool for securing a ski is an obvious choice: The ski vice. The ski vice is made to secure

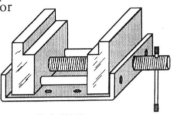

the ski tightly while leaving the base completely accessible for

Single Ski Vice

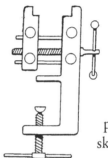

repairs. Some ski vices are made to mount to a work bench permanently, while others are portable. A good single or double ski vice from a ski shop can be well worth the cost.

Portable Ski Vice

The All-Purpose Bench Vice

One alternative to the ski vice is an all-purpose bench vice. Use a soft material for padding between the ski and the vice's jaws to protect the side walls, base and top skin of the ski. Also, support the ski underneath, at both the tip and tail sections, with two wooden blocks wrapped in cloth.

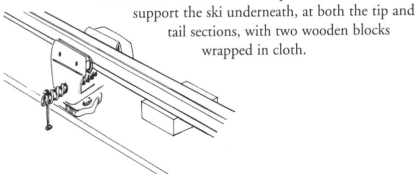

Retracting Ski Brakes

One of many ways to secure ski brakes out of the way while tuning is to use thick rubber bands. Simply retract the brakes, then loop one end of the rubber band around one of the brake arms. Now pull the rubber band up and over the binding housing, then down to hook around the other brake arm. You may have to wrap it twice to hold the retracted brakes securely.

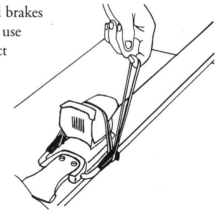

Strong nylon string in place of the rubber band also works well for securing ski brakes.

TUNER'S TIP NO. 2
"Practice Makes Perfect Cents."

Before you begin working on your own set of premium skis, you may want to practice a few times on a set of expendable skis that you are not afraid to damage, especially for the edge sharpening process. If you don't have a used pair of alpine skis laying around in the basement or garage, you might consider buying an old set from a ski shop, or through the classified ads. You could find this $30 to $40 to be a good investment and a great learning tool.

Tuner's Checklist:

☑ Properly padded jaws of the bench vice.

☑ Vice is secure on bench at a comfortable height.

☑ Ski Brakes and all other obstructions are removed from above the plane of the ski base for smooth, uninterrupted tool action over the base.

Dirt, wear and tear and gouging in bases can significantly decrease ski performance. In this section, you will learn to treat each of these problems in order to keep your skis in peak-performance condition.

Base Cleaning

Once you have secured the ski, the next step is to clean the base in preparation for tuning. Since a ski base is made up of porous material, especially so in the case of sintered bases, you will need to use a cleaning solution in order to remove grit and grime from the base.

Solvents and Other Cleaning Agents

If there is grit and grime on the ski base, don't scrape it off with a metal or plastic scraper, as this may permanently embed the debris into the base material. Instead, first use a clean shop cloth or paper towel and wax remover, denatured alcohol, mineral spirits, or other mild solvent to clean up dirt, grime and wax residue from the base. Probably the least expensive,

TUNER'S TIP NO. 3

"Get Some Air."

Be certain that your work area is well-ventilated, especially when using cleaning solvents. Proper ventilation will also protect you from wax smoke when hot-waxing your skis. Both solvent fumes and wax smoke can be hazardous if breathed and can cause irritation to eyes and nasal passages.

safest, yet very effective cleaning agent is isopropyl alcohol, which is simply household rubbing alcohol. It evaporates quickly and leaves very little residue.

Evaporation Time

Once you have cleaned the base thoroughly, wipe it down with a paper towel or shop rag and allow it to dry for at least 10 minutes. If you have a build up of wax on the base, use wax remover and follow the instructions on the can.

Truing the Base

Through wear and tear, aging or continual machine tuning, a ski base may lose its flat contour. Check the base for trueness, or flatness, before making any base repairs.

Base Contour Conditions

There are basically three contour conditions that a ski base can assume:

Flat— The base is even with the edges.
Convex— The base is higher than the edges.
Concave— The base is lower than the edges.

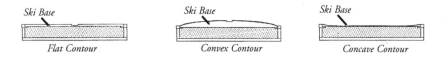

Ski Base	Ski Base	Ski Base
Flat Contour	Convex Contour	Concave Contour

The best way to determine the contour condition of a ski base is to view the ski lengthwise at eye-level from the tip or the tail. Place the true bar across the ski base and use background lighting to enhance the view. If the base is concave, light can be seen under the true bar at the center por-

Light

tion of the base. If the base is convex, you will see more light through the areas at the two outer edges of the base and less toward the center. And finally, if the base is flat, you will see little or no light between the base and the true bar.

If there are varied contours along the length of the ski base, use a felt-tip marker on the metal edge of the ski to identify these isolated areas. This will give you an accurate indication of where the base and/or edge need the most work.

A flat ski base is the most desirable contour condition for the average skier. Occasionally, competitive racers desire a convex base in certain snow conditions, as more base and less edge on the snow results in faster skis. A convex base may also make it easier to initiate turns, but carries the disadvantage of being much harder to control because the ski tends to sway and lose tracking. For the needs of the average skier, flat is best for control, efficiency of motion and overall skiability.

Treatment of Convex Base

The tools and procedures used to flatten a convex ski base vary. Through experimentation and practical testing, you will be able determine which of the following methods works best for you.

Metal Scraper Method

Hold the scraper in both hands with your fingers over the top for downward pressure and your thumbs near the bottom, pointing toward each other while applying forward, lateral pressure. Now lean the top of the scraper blade away from you about 20 to 25 degrees. Spreading your thumbs as far apart as possible will help to keep the scraper level, ensuring even and consistent removal of base material. While resting the scraper on the base, push the scraper from the tip to the tail with smooth, comfortable strokes, overlapping each pass. The amount of downward pressure you apply onto the base of the ski with the scraper should be determined by whatever pressure is needed to remove a moderate amount of base material in one stroke over the base. Use caution here not to damage the metal edge with the scraper. Also, as you scrape the base, frequently use the true bar to monitor developing flatness.

TUNER'S TIP NO. 4

"Steeper is Sharper!"

With the tip of the scraper blade filed squarely, the steeper (or closer to vertical) angle you use while scraping, the more base material the scraper will remove. If you scrape with an angle too close to horizontal, the blade will skid over the base inefficiently and remove little material.

TUNER'S TIP NO. 5

"Don't be Dull!"

The scraper should be kept extremely sharp at all times because a dull scraper may burnish (close pores) the base material and hinder wax penetration.

Sandpaper Method

Another way to flatten a convex base is to use a medium grit silicon carbide sandpaper wrapped around a firm sanding block. Apply consistent downward and forward pressure onto the sanding block and brush the base from tip to tail in smooth, overlapping strokes. The longest and stiffest of your mill bastard files may also be used as a sanding block. As you sand the base down, frequently check your work with your true bar.

Pansar Blade Method

The pansar blade is another tool you can use to flatten the base of your ski. It tends to shave away the base material, instead of tearing or peeling it. Simply place the pansar blade across the ski base at about a 30 degree angle. Apply all the pressure with your palm directly on top of the blade in the center of the base and draw it from tip to tail in smooth, overlapping strokes. Remember to frequently check your work with a true bar.

Treatment of Concave Base

Initiating even the slightest turns can be quite difficult when the base of the ski is concave because the edges are grabbing and hooking in the snow.

Once you have determined with your true bar that the base is concave, file the edges and outer base area down evenly on both sides until they are level with the lowest point of the concave base. For instructions on filing, refer to Section IV: *Sharpening Ski Edges*.

Filling In Gouges

Obstacles like rocks and branches are simply a part of skiing. Though they can often be avoided, occasional abrasions from these hazards are inevitable. Gradually, if left untreated, these rocks and

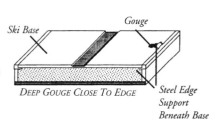

Ski Base   *Gouge*

DEEP GOUGE CLOSE TO EDGE

Steel Edge Support Beneath Base

branches can gouge away the base of your ski. And a deep enough gouge close to the edge of your ski may allow water to penetrate to the steel edge support that lies beneath the base. This could cause irreparable rust and/or delamination of the base material.

If you encounter a gouge that is deep enough to expose the core material or steel edge support just beneath the base of the ski, take it to a ski shop and request that the technician weld the base with a hot-air welder. You will find this well worth the cost because a conventional application of melted P-tex on a deep gouge is not likely to last and could even worsen the problem by blistering the base material around the gouge.

Gouge Contamination

Whenever you encounter a gouge, assume it is contaminated.  Whether it be dirt, oil, wax residue, or any other foreign substance that comes in contact with the base of your ski, it should be thoroughly removed. One of the major causes of mis-bonded P-tex is gouge contamination.

Some technicians prefer to use soap and water, a clean towel and a fine wire brush to clean the gouge. The wire brush not only helps to loosen and lift foreign material from the gouge, but also gives it a rough texture, allowing the P-tex to bond even tighter. You can also use a toothbrush with rubbing alcohol to clean out the gouges. Almost any tool that scrubs and reaches deep into the gouge to clean will work well.

TUNER'S TIP NO. 6

"Cool is Clean is Cool."

An additional way to keep carbon from building up on the burning P-tex is to store it in the freezer until you are ready to use it. The colder temperature reduces the rate at which carbon will form.

Application of P-tex

Make certain that the entire base is dry before you apply P-tex. **P-tex will not adhere well to a gouge holding moisture.** To ensure a good bond, allow the area to dry for about 10 to 15 minutes after cleaning. Swabbing it with a paper towel will absorb excess moisture and speed this process.

P-tex—basically the same polyethylene material that your ski base is made of—comes in the form of a stick (or candle) about the size and shape of a thick pencil. Be sure to choose black P-tex for a black ski base and clear P-tex for a clear, or multi-colored base.

P-tex Candle Only Method (No Torch)

The idea here is to ignite the tip of the P-tex candle and allow it to burn itself, then drip it into gouges in the base.

First, light the tip of the P-tex candle and allow it to drip onto your metal scraper. As you will see, a large, yellow flame on the tip of the candle will produce a build-up of undesirable black carbon flakes on the outer surface of the liquified P-tex. This is not only unsightly, but carbon also inhibits the bonding capability of the P-tex. **P-tex should drip into the gouge clean and carbon-free.**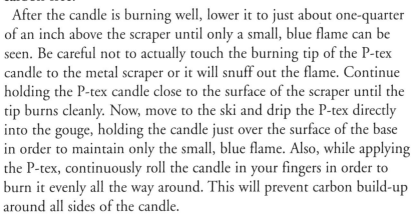

After the candle is burning well, lower it to just about one-quarter of an inch above the scraper until only a small, blue flame can be seen. Be careful not to actually touch the burning tip of the P-tex candle to the metal scraper or it will snuff out the flame. Continue holding the P-tex candle close to the surface of the scraper until the tip burns cleanly. Now, move to the ski and drip the P-tex directly into the gouge, holding the candle just over the surface of the base in order to maintain only the small, blue flame. Also, while applying the P-tex, continuously roll the candle in your fingers in order to burn it evenly all the way around. This will prevent carbon build-up around all sides of the candle.

As you drip a bead of hot P-tex into a deep gouge, do not apply too much in one spot at a time. It may not dry properly beneath the surface if it is too thick in one place.

Take your time when making the P-tex application, especially when you are just learning this step. You can always go back and drip more P-tex into a gouge, once the first layer is completely cool and dry. Finally, make sure that you use plenty of P-tex, overflowing each gouge to ensure full coverage.

While applying P-tex, keep your metal scraper nearby in the other hand so that you can move your P-tex candle away from the gouge and back to the scraper quickly, should black carbon reappear. This also helps as you transfer the burning P-tex candle over to the next gouge in the base, or if you need to snuff the end of the candle out by laying it directly onto the metal scraper. If carbon begins to reappear on the tip of the P-tex candle, remove it from above the ski immediately and move it to the metal scraper, as before, until the tip of the candle burns clean again. Once the tip clears, you may return to the ski.

The Torch Method

Some ski technicians prefer to use a small butane or propane torch to heat P-tex. It takes time to master this technique, but after some practice, you may find it goes even faster than other methods and produces a cleaner, steadier bead of P-tex.

To begin this process, light your torch and adjust the flame to a medium or low setting. Too much flame can not only be dangerous, but it may also burn too much P-tex at once and cause you to lose control of the bead dripping onto the ski.

With the P-tex candle in one hand and a small, hand-held torch in the other, burn the end of the candle and drip it onto a metal scraper until it burns clean and clear. At that point, you may move to the ski and begin dripping P-tex into the gouges. Remember to continuously rotate the P-tex candle as you work and keep the flame of the torch on the tip of the candle in order to keep carbon from building up. Be sure to turn the flame upwards when working near the ski base to avoid scorching.

Again, in deeper gouges, you may find that the P-tex doesn't fill the entire depth with one pass. Wait until the first layer of P-tex is cool and dry, then return to the gouge to add another layer. Continue this until the gouge is filled.

NOTE: **Refer to Appendix B for special considerations regarding P-tex application on sintered bases.**

Removal of P-tex

There are several different methods of removing P-tex from a ski base. Through experimentation and practice, you will be able to determine which method best suits you.

Once all the gouges are filled, allow the P-tex to cool for at least 15 to 20 minutes. If you are repairing one ski at a time, this is a good opportunity to begin filling in the gouges on the other ski. A longer cooling time ensures that the bond to the ski base is complete and that the P-tex has stiffened enough for easy removal.

The first step of P-tex removal is getting the excess P-tex shaved down nearly flush with the surface of the base.

Surform® Blade Method

A Surform® blade works well for removal of excess P-tex, but you should be very careful to keep the blade level with the base surface to avoid damaging the base.

First, lightly and with very smooth, deliberate strokes, pass the Surform® blade over the protruding P-tex until the lump is nearly flush with the base. **In this procedure, it is most important to work gradually.** Afterwards, finish smoothing out the repair with 400+ grit silicon carbide sandpaper.

Razor Blade Method

A razor blade is also a very efficient tool for removing excess P-tex. Use a small handle that is designed to accommodate single edge razor blades for added control and support. In much the same way as a razor blade, a sharp wood chisel also works very well for removing excess P-tex.

Pansar Blade Method

You may also use a pansar blade for the removal of excess P-tex. Simply rest the pansar on the base over the P-tex and press down firmly on top of the blade with the palm of your hand while pulling or pushing it over the lump of P-tex.

After shaving off the excess P-tex with any of the methods mentioned, you can use 400+ grit silicon carbide sandpaper and a sanding block to smooth these areas in the base completely with a final, light sanding.

Tuner's Checklist

☑ Properly removed all debris from base, cleaned and allowed solvent to dry before tuning.

☑ Ski base checked for trueness and corrected if necessary.

☑ Gouges in ski base cleaned properly and filled with P-tex, then scraped flush with base material.

SHARPENING SKI EDGES

Once you have completed all of the base repairs and sufficiently flattened the ski base, it is time to break out your files and begin the edge repairs and sharpening. This should be done about every 10 to 15 skiing days.

The base should already be free of any debris or residue, but check it again just to be sure. Nothing is more frustrating than old wax residue and base shavings gumming up the file.

NOTE: **If you wish to file a bevel into the edge of your ski, read through both the flat-filing and beveling steps before beginning file work.**

Flat-Filing the Edge

You will find the 12-inch, 10-inch and 8-inch mill bastard files to be some of the most essential tools for tuning skis. Mastering their use is developed only through patience and lots of practice. You will know that you are becoming proficient when you can initiate productive cutting stokes with smooth, seemingly effortless flow. But remember, that takes time!

When just learning the art of ski tuning, you may want to use the medium to smaller length files. Larger files have larger blades and cut more material away per stroke. But for doing low volume work at home, it is best to stick with the 12-inch or 10-inch mill bastard file for the beginning edge repair work and an 8-inch file for the smoother, more delicate finishing work. It is also particularly important here to take your time because over-filing the edge can cause undue wear and shorten the life of your ski.

Also, make certain that the ski is secure in the vice. The ability to apply pressure with your file, both downward and laterally onto the ski, with little or no movement of the ski, is essential for a quality tune-up.

Sharpening Bottom Edges

Make a thorough investigation of both edges and get an overall idea of the kind of work that needs to be done. For instance, you may notice some isolated rough spots on the edge from encounters with rocks, branches and other hazards. Before starting to file the entire ski edge, smooth out these rough spots by drawing your mill bastard file over them once or twice.

Mill Bastard File Method

Place your mill bastard file on the ski and find the angle of the file on the edge that most efficiently shaves the metal edge—usually about 30 to 45 degrees. Hold the file with the tang (pointed) end away from the cutting direction. For example, if you plan to draw the file toward you, you would want the tang end of the file to point to the tip—away from you—since you would be tuning from tip to tail.

Apply pressure to one edge at a time while drawing the file toward you. Too much downward pressure, though, will likely cause it to chatter, or skip along the edge. Too little pressure and the file will not remove enough edge to make a difference. You must experiment in order to get a feel for the most efficient amount of pressure to be used. Also, during this process, try not to bend the file too much for the obvious dangers of breaking the file or unintentionally beveling the edge.

Begin each stroke with very little downward pressure, then gradually increase the pressure until you feel the file cut the metal edge. This resistance will naturally force you to increase the lateral force to maintain a steady stroke. Complete each overlapping stroke as gradually as you began— move into the stroke slowly and smoothly, and out in the same manner.

To make the process easier and more efficient, keep the downward pressure directly beneath your shoulders and hold the file flat on the edge, without rocking it from side to side. Start at the tip of the ski and begin filing toward the tail in sections of about a foot or so, or whatever length is most comfortable and enables you to implement smooth, steady, overlapping strokes. Remember to concentrate with pressure on one edge at a time.

Any unnatural movement while filing may result in an uneven or rough edge surface. After practicing with the file, you will soon develop a feel for the pressure required to efficiently remove the metal, yet still maintain smooth cuts. Always move in and out of each stroke carefully and smoothly, yet with confidence. After you have completed filing, always polish the edge with 400+ grit sandpaper wrapped around a sanding block or file.

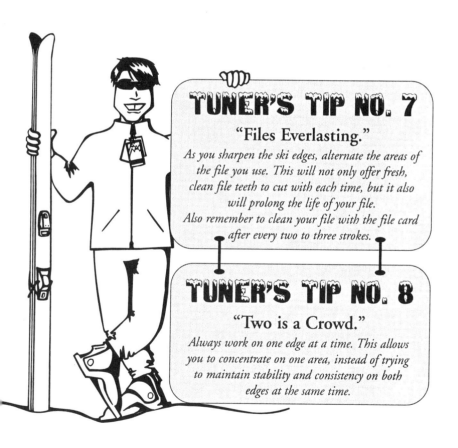

TUNER'S TIP NO. 7
"Files Everlasting."
As you sharpen the ski edges, alternate the areas of the file you use. This will not only offer fresh, clean file teeth to cut with each time, but it also will prolong the life of your file.
Also remember to clean your file with the file card after every two to three strokes.

TUNER'S TIP NO. 8
"Two is a Crowd."
Always work on one edge at a time. This allows you to concentrate on one area, instead of trying to maintain stability and consistency on both edges at the same time.

Edge Sharpening Tool Method

There are a variety of compact, hand-held edge sharpening tools that are specifically designed for the job, and many are relatively inexpensive in proportion to the amount of time and trouble that they can save you. Since there are so many styles of edge sharpening tools available, only a general explanation of their use will be covered here.

Basically, the edge sharpening tool is a small, hand-held device equipped with a carbide blade or file section. One portion of the tool is designed to ride along the side wall and/or base of the ski as the blade shaves the edge. The cuts are very clean and accurate, and many models require only a simple knob adjustment in order to change the degree of bevel. You should still use a mill bastard file to smooth out rough spots on the edge prior to using the edge sharpening tool.

If you choose to use an edge sharpening tool, be sure to follow the instructions that come with your specific model of tool to ensure best results.

Sharpening Side Edges

After the bottom edges have been sharpened, place the ski in the vice on its edge. Be certain that it is secured, blocked and padded. Now, rest the file lengthwise on the side edge of the ski with the tang end away from the cutting direction. You might notice that without the wide support of the entire base of the ski, the file tends to rock from side to side. One way to eliminate that is to use a small block of wood (2-inch by 4-inch cut to about 4-5 inches in length) for added support. Place the wooden block flat on the base of the ski and, again, place the file lengthwise on the edge, with one side resting on the ski's side edge and the other side on the wooden block. There is now a stable platform for the file, enabling it to ride smoothly and evenly on the side edge. This will ensure a plumb cut and a consistently smooth, sharp edge.

De-Burring Edges

As you sharpen, tiny burrs are formed on the edges. De-burring the edges with an emery cloth, a whet stone, or 400+ grit sandpaper is a necessary final step to provide the smoothest glide possible.

Whatever you use, be certain that it is not a coarse material. After spending a significant amount of your time sharpening the edge of your ski, you don't want to lose the keenness of the edge by pressing too hard, or by using coarse material to de-burr.

This process is relatively easy. Simply run the de-burring material lightly up and down the entire length of each edge once or twice to remove any metal burrs left from sharpening.

De-Tuning Edges

The idea behind de-tuning is to actually remove a bit of the sharpness from the edges at the tip and tail sections of your skis just enough to make initiating turns easier. If the tip and tail sections are too sharp, you may find that the skis feel "grabby" or difficult to control because the edges tend to catch on the snow.

To de-tune your skis, brush the edges with a whet stone or rubber gummy stone just a few inches down from the tip of the ski through the shovel and a few inches up from the tail. This is done in much the same way as deburring. The difference is when you are de-tuning you are actually dulling the edge slightly by applying more pressure, not just removing burrs.

There are many variations of de-tuning, each an attempt to obtain the best possible edge configuration for individual skier. Some like more, or longer, de-tuning on the edge, others prefer less. Experiment to find the most effective amount of tip and tail dulling for you. The general idea is to avoid hooking an edge in the snow from overly-sharp tip and tail sections, yet to maintain a sharp edge through the center of the ski to ensure responsive turns and control.

Beveling the Edges

Today, the treatment of beveling edges has become the status quo. The question of whether or not to bevel is seldom asked. Instead, it is now, "To what degree should one bevel?"

Beveling is the process of filing the edges of a ski on a slant, thus allowing less edge to remain in contact with the snow. This improves glide, lessens the chance of catching edges and provides smoother turn initiation and transition. Generally, with edges beveled slightly, skis tend to be easier to maneuver and control. However, you may not want to bevel edges if conditions are icy or hard-packed. For obvious reasons, when conditions are icy, it is best to have as much edge on the snow as possible.

One rule of thumb is to always field test your skis first, then gradually increase bevel only as needed. If you are sure the base is flat and you have sufficiently de-tuned the edges, but your skis still tend to catch edges or hesitate when you begin to initiate a turn, you may need to increase bevel slightly.

Soon, after trial and error, you will be able to determine which degree of bevel best suits you and your personal style of skiing in various snow conditions. For the average skier, edges should be beveled somewhere between 1/2 and 2 degrees. Any greater degree of bevel may hinder your control of the ski. You can always file more off of the edge, but it is obviously impossible to add on. Always begin with a 1/2-degree bevel or less.

> **NOTE: You should not bevel in addition to flat-filing the ski edge! As you apply a bevel, you are actually sharpening the edge simultaneously.**

Beveling Bottom Edges

Beveling the bottom edges requires the same procedure as flat-filing your skis, the only difference is that the portion of the file that rides on top of the opposite edge during the filing process is elevated slightly. The leaning posture of the file actually produces the bevel, or slant, on the edge of the ski. So, basically, you already know how to bevel; there is just one detail left—tilting the file.

Mill Bastard File Method

Begin beveling by placing your mill bastard file over the ski at the most efficient cutting angle—generally about 30 to 45 degrees—as

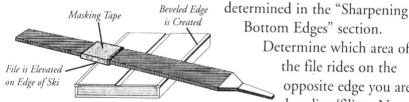

Masking Tape

Beveled Edge is Created

File is Elevated on Edge of Ski

determined in the "Sharpening Bottom Edges" section. Determine which area of the file rides on the opposite edge you are beveling/filing. Now, wrap masking tape around your mill bastard file two to three times at that point. You have just raised the file up on the opposite edge of the ski enough to achieve about 1/2 to 1 degree of bevel on the edge you are filing. Four to five wraps around the file approximate 1-1/2 to 2 degrees of bevel. Fine sandpaper may be substituted for the masking tape if you want to polish the opposite edge of the ski while you bevel.

After beveling a ski, always check it with your true bar to make sure that the angle of bevel is consistent throughout the entire length of the ski. With back-lighting, look beneath the true bar positioned directly over the edge. You will now be able to judge the angle of the bevel by comparing it to the angle and amount of light shining between the true bar and the beveled edge.

There are also various edge beveling tools on the market today. Most are adjustable, offering you a consistent and precise degree of bevel every time. Check with any ski shop as to the brands and prices of these tools.

TUNER'S TIP NO. 10

"Savings Goes Both Ways."

In order to reduce undue wear on the edge, as well as save effort and time, you can prolong the sharpness of a beveled edge by simply sharpening only the side edge of the ski periodically.

One recommended alternative to using masking tape to elevate the file is to use beveling sleeves. These inexpensive accessories are designed to slip over a file and raise the part that rides on the opposite edge just enough to implement the proper degree of bevel. The various thicknesses and colors represent different degrees of bevel and allow you to hand-file a bevel with even greater accuracy and consistency. These beveling sleeves can be found at your local ski shop and could prove to be an invaluable investment.

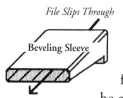

File Slips Through

Beveling Sleeve

Edge Sharpening Tool Method

As mentioned in Section IV: *Sharpening Ski Edges.*, many edge sharpening tools are equipped with a simple adjustment knob to change the degree of bevel from 0 to 3 degrees. Again, you should still use the mill bastard file to smooth out rough spots on the edge prior to using the edge sharpening tool.

If you choose to use an edge sharpening tool, be sure to follow the instructions that come with your specific model of tool to ensure the best results.

Beveling Side Edges

A side-edge bevel has also become another commonly practiced tuning treatment. If you spend a lot of time skiing when conditions are icy and need a full 90-degrees of edge digging into the surface, you may want to consider employing a side-edge bevel.

Edge

Ski Base

Unfortunately, there is really no efficient way to incorporate a bevel into a side edge by hand unless you have a tool specifically designed for the job. There are a number of side edge beveling tools on the market today, so inquire at any ski shop as to brands and models of these job-specific tools. Again, be sure to follow the instructions that come with your specific model and tool to ensure best results.

Tuner's Checklist

☑ Files cleaned and sharpened, ready for action.

☑ Bottom and side edges sharpened, deburred and de-tuned according to procedure.

☑ If desired, edges beveled. (Edges sharpened through this procedure)

V | STRUCTURING THE BASE

Everyone seems to agree that base structuring greatly improves the glide of skis over the surface of the snow. The fundamental intent of structuring is to score the base material with tiny lines and patterned deviations that allow air and water to displace more freely beneath the surface of the ski base, thereby reducing friction and drag. This disruption relieves the pressure, or vacuum, underneath the ski and dramatically improves glide.

Methods of Structuring

First, make sure you have completed all base cleaning and repairs and that you have filed the edges before you begin structuring. Any base or edge work done afterwards will obviously reduce structure.

A simple rule to follow in structuring is: **The wetter the snow, the rougher the base structure.** That makes sense because in wet snow, a thicker film of water is formed under the base of the ski, which requires larger channels to enter and escape.

Riller Bar Method

Use of a riller bar (or rilling tool) is probably the cleanest and most trouble-free method of structuring. A riller bar, which is usually equipped with a coarse side and a finer side, will actually cut grooves into the base, leaving clean, nearly fiber-free channels. Practice rilling on a set of expendable skis before you start on your premium set of skis, though. That way, you will get an idea of how much pressure is required to cut sufficient grooves in the base.

With both hands over the riller bar and just outside the edges of the ski, hold it steady and begin pulling it from the tip of the ski toward the tail with downward pressure. A continuous draw through the entire length of the ski is best. And once or twice down the entire length of the ski is enough. Next, use a scouring pad or a fine, brass-bristle brush to remove debris from the grooves and to direct any fibers left from the rilling process toward the tail of the ski.

Sandpaper Method

Sandpaper is a simple, inexpensive material you can use for structuring. A synthetic silicon carbide sandpaper, 180 to 120-grit is best for cold, mid-winter snow. And 120 to 100-grit works well for average snow conditions, while spring skiing would likely require 100 to 80-grit sandpaper.

Simply wrap a section of sandpaper around a file or sanding block. Sand the base in long, overlapping intervals from tip to tail, while applying enough downward pressure to significantly score the base material. The same rules of maintaining smooth, overlapping parallel strokes apply here, just as in flat-filing.

Repeat sanding the length of the ski 2 to 3 times. It is important to remember that when you structure using sandpaper, you produce significantly more fibers than when you use a riller bar. The riller bar cleanly cuts grooves into the base, as opposed to the sandpaper, which tends to tear the base material.

Now that you have produced hundreds of tiny groves in the base, clean them free of sanding dust and other debris by using a stiff toothbrush, brass-bristle brush or scouring pad. Remember to follow the same pattern during cleaning that you used to structure the base with sandpaper so that the small fibers that are formed may either be removed, or become redirected toward the tail of the ski.

Metal Scraper Method

Sharpen the metal scraper once again, but this time do not de-burr the edges. To apply structure, run the scraper straight down the base of the ski from tip to tail once or twice. With the burrs left on the scraper, tiny lines are scribed into the base of the ski, leaving a very fine structure pattern behind. Remember to lean the scraper toward you if you are drawing it, or away from you if you are pushing it over the base.

Afterward, remember to clean out the grooves in the base and set any resulting fibers from tip to tail using a toothbrush, scouring pad, or brass-bristle brush.

> **NOTE:** The burred metal scraper method is only applicable for the coldest snow conditions, since it will leave only a fine structure.

Trying New Patterns of Structuring

Once you have gained some proficiency at structuring, you may want to score some diagonal lines or other patterns into the ski base. Try structuring at various increments in the base, leaving some sections smooth and unstructured. You may even try varying grits of silicon carbide sandpaper at different areas on the base. Experiment with these patterns until you find one or two structure patterns that work best for you.

NOTES

Tuner's Checklist

☑ All base repairs completed, base cleaned, edge work finished.

☑ Base structured according to one of methods described.

☑ Experiment with new patterns of structuring.

Ski waxes come in many colors, shapes and sizes, each formulated for a specific snow condition—everything from ice to slush. The fact is, an all-temperature ski wax performs well in most snow conditions. In the case of very extreme conditions, though, you may want to purchase a temperature-specific wax. Consult with a ski shop before purchasing a temperature-specific wax to ensure you are getting just what you need.

Applying Wax

Ironing the ski wax into a ski's porous base ensures that it penetrates the base material for the best possible coverage and ski glide.

If your skis are iron waxed, the wax will wear down about every 3 skiing days. If the wax is rubbed on, you'll need to reapply it every day. Mark the difference in glide from when the skis are freshly waxed and then 3 days later. In most cases, no matter what the snow conditions, you will likely notice a difference.

TUNER'S TIP NO. 11
"Waxed For Action"

Ideally, skis should be waxed every one to two skiing days, as waxing is one of the most important factors to influence the overall performance of the skis.

First, warm the iron to medium heat. Do not heat the iron to a temperature that causes the wax to smoke heavily on the surface of the iron, because too much heat can break down the wax's chemical properties.

Once the iron is fully heated, hold it tip-down over the ski base, apply the wax to the hot iron surface and allow it to drip off the pointed tip of the iron onto the base. As soon as the wax begins dripping from the iron, run a bead down the length of the ski base twice—down one side and up the other. An S-shaped pattern, down once and up again, also works well for distributing the right amount of wax onto the base.

Once you have dripped the wax onto the base, iron it in, covering the entire base. Continue ironing the wax into the base for about five minutes. Remember to turn the temperature down a bit if at any time you see heavy smoke rising from the surface of the iron. Once you have completely saturated the base, allow it to cool for at least 15 to 20 minutes. While one ski is cooling, use the time to begin waxing the mate.

> **NOTE:** Refer to Appendix B for special considerations of waxing a sintered base.

Removing Wax

After the wax has cooled, use your plastic scraper to remove the excess surface wax. Lean the top of the scraper away from you and push it over the base from tip to tail. Use your thumbs at the bottom of the scraper for forward, lateral force and your fingers over the top of the scraper for light, downward pressure. Now, scrape off the excess wax using smooth, overlapping, comfortable length strokes. Don't remove too much wax at once, but scrape it off in degrees until only a thin, invisible layer of wax remains.

Once you have removed the excess wax from the base of the ski, be certain that the side walls and edges are free of wax drippings. And if your ski base has a center groove, you will also need a popsicle stick, flattened on one end to clean out the groove.

Post-Wax Structuring

Once you have completed waxing and scraping, clean out the wax from the structure grooves using a toothbrush. Remember to brush from tip to tail. After that, use a scouring pad to smooth out rough spots and create a final fine-structured surface on the waxed base.

Tuner's Checklist

- ☑ Consult ski shop as to best wax for extreme snow conditions.
- ☑ Iron ski wax into base according to procedure described.
- ☑ Scrape wax with plastic scraper, leaving a thin, invisible layer.
- ☑ Post-wax structuring, or buffing is completed.

VII | BINDING MAINTENANCE

Since the boot and binding system is the only mechanical, moving part of your equipment, great care is required to maintain the integrity and safety of boot release and retention.

Basic Maintenance At Home

It is important to have a certified ski binding technician check your bindings at least once per year. But there are a number of maintenance tasks you can perform at home to ensure that your bindings are consistently operating at peak performance. Below, you will find important instructions to keep your bindings retaining and releasing smoothly.

Cleaning

The first step in cleaning your bindings is to completely wipe the exterior surface of the binding housing with a clean shop towel, then you may clean the internal working parts of the binding. Use that same clean shop towel wrapped around a thin, stiff object to help you reach the inner parts of the binding. You may want to use a popsickle stick for this purpose. Simply remove the dirt and grime from those working parts as best you can, then lubricate.

Lubrication

All accessible moving parts on the binding should be lubricated with binding grease or spray lubricant each year for maximum safety and accurate binding performance. In order to help you reach those tight spots inside the binding housing, again, use a popsickle stick, or other thin instrument to apply stiffened grease to those areas and wipe off the excess. Your local ski shop can provide you with information about some specialized lubricants that resist water and corrosion—best for binding maintenance.

Boot/Binding System Safety

The sole purpose of a ski binding system is to hold, or "bind", you securely on the skis until the point of lateral and/or vertical pressure **43** occurs that will likely exceed a safe and comfortable level of boot retention. A properly maintained binding system is designed to release just before you reach that level. Here are some tips to keep that system operating safely.

Needed Precautions

Even through normal use, various parts of a the boot/binding release system may naturally lose some of their performance characteristics. One of these is the anti-friction device, or AFD, installed on the binding toe beneath boot toe area. This AFD provides a smooth, slick surface to enable the boot toe to move out of the binding more easily upon release. After some time the AFD may become worn and scratched, resulting in more friction between boot and binding, and less consistent release. Be sure to keep an eye on this area and ask your ski technician to advise you as to when to replace the AFD.

> **NOTE:** "Accurate binding release" refers to the binding's capability of releasing you when necessary in the event of a fall. Both pre-release and failed release are undesirable and dangerous.

Boots are also subject to extreme wear and tear, and accurate binding release is greatly affected by the shape and texture of the boot toe and heel. This should always be considered when testing the function of a binding.

Calibration

Over the course of time and use, ski boots and bindings may not perform as well as they might have when they were new. Springs in bindings may become weaker, rivets on moving parts might stiffen, and boots become worn and more or less resistant to release. In order to maintain accurately timed release from the binding and to ensure your own safety, these boot/binding systems must be tested periodically according to a standard of force measurements. This testing and readjustment of boot/binding systems to maintain accurate release is known as calibration. Ski technicians, with the proper tools and skills, can accurately judge the amount of force necessary

> **NOTE:** You should have your bindings calibrated at least once a year, or as often as you require any readjustment or maintenance of your bindings—whichever comes first.

to release your boot from your binding. If the force required to release your boot from your binding exceeds, or falls below the standard given for your weight, height, etc., then the technician must readjust your binding retention settings to compensate.

Storage

Proper storage in the off-season and during travel is important if you want your bindings to last a long time. Here are some tips for the road and otherwise.

Stowage During Travel

When transporting skis atop an automobile, binding covers are essential to preserve the long life of your bindings. Road

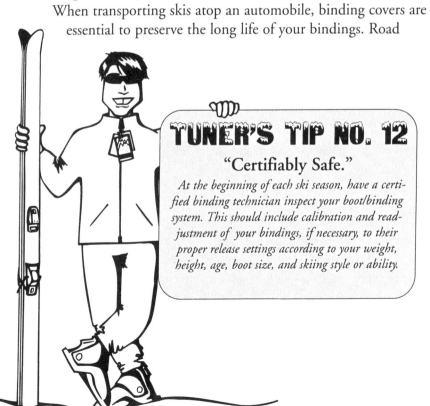

TUNER'S TIP NO. 12
"Certifiably Safe."

At the beginning of each ski season, have a certified binding technician inspect your boot/binding system. This should include calibration and readjustment of your bindings, if necessary, to their proper release settings according to your weight, height, age, boot size, and skiing style or ability.

salts, dirt, and other foreign materials can penetrate into the binding housing during transport and hinder smooth operation of moving parts deep within the bindings' mechanisms.

Summer Storage

At the end of each ski season, you may want to turn down the binding retention springs to their minimum settings. This will help to maintain the integrity of the spring by relieving the tension throughout the off-season. Whether you chose to do this or not, you should, at the beginning of the next ski season, employ a certified binding technician to inspect, calibrate and readjust your bindings, if necessary, to their proper release settings according to your weight, height, age, boot size and skiing style or ability. This will ensure your utmost safety. A certified binding technician has been trained in troubleshooting, proper binding adjustment procedures and setting correct tension settings using up-to-date charts.

Tuner's Checklist

☑ Bindings cleaned and lubricated.

☑ Professional check-up and maintenance performed, including calibration.

☑ Proper stowage during travel.

☑ Proper storage of ski equipment during off season.

CONCLUSION

Congratulations on a job well done! Now that you have completed tuning your own skis, the fun has only begun. Through personal experience, you will continue to learn much more about skis, ski tuning, and what makes a ski perform well. No doubt you will develop many of your own methods of tuning suited to your own needs and style. The more you field test your own tune-ups practically on the slopes, the more you will enjoy keeping your skis in top-performance condition. And no matter where your skiing adventures may take you, always maintain the essence of the sport—having fun From Tip to Tail!

APPENDIX A

Maintenance of Metal Scraper

A sharp scraper is as important to a ski technician as a sharp scalpel is to a surgeon. To maintain the edge, you can sharpen the scraper by laying your 10-inch or 12-inch mill bastard file on a flat surface with the tang (pointed) end butted against a sturdy, vertical surface for a backboard. Place the scraper perpendicular and lengthwise onto the file, and keep the scraper at a 90-degree angle to the file surface. Now,

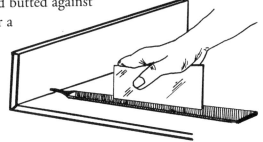

using smooth, forward strokes with light downward pressure, begin honing down the scraper.

The idea is to make the bottom edge surface of the scraper as flat as possible. Several passes over the file should be sufficient to give you two sharp edges to be used alternately.

Finally, de-burr the edges of the scraper lightly with 400+ grit silicon carbide sandpaper.

Maintenance of Plastic Scraper

The same care is required for a plastic scraper as is for a metal scraper, with one additional procedure: Before using the plastic scraper, especially when removing wax, brush the flat edge over fine sandpaper on a flat surface several times to remove any scrawling from the teeth of the file and any other rough spots. Continue to keep the scraper at a 90-degree angle to the sandpaper at all times to insure the sharpest edge. Then, remove burrs with at least 400-grit sandpaper.

Maintenance of File Card

Draw a fine-tooth hair comb through the file card periodically to keep it free of debris like base material or wax build-up.

Maintenance of Mill Bastard Files

Keep files free of debris between the blades using a file card before, during and after ski tuning. This process is essential to maintain quality ski tune-ups.

Always store files separately and in an upright position, or laying flat with each file wrapped individually in thick paper towels or cloth. Stacking files uncovered is the surest way to cause untimely dulling.

Maintenance of Edge Sharpening Tool

As you sharpen with an edging tool, tiny metal shavings inevitably build up on the blade. Keep this as clean as possible. It may require you to clear out shavings after each stroke.

Maintenance of Pansar Blade

Like the mill bastard file, keep the pansar blade free of debris between the blades by using a file card before, during and after ski tuning.

Maintenance of True Bar

Keep the true bar clean with solvent and a clean shop towel in order to avoid any false readings.

Maintenance of Brass-Bristle Brush

Draw a fine-tooth hair comb through the bristles periodically to keep it free of debris like base material or wax build-up.

Maintenance of Riller Bar

Keep the riller bar clean with a file card for clean structure patterns.

Maintenance of Surform®Tool

Keep the blades of the Surform® clear of debris to allow for clean, consistent cutting action. Toothpicks work very well for this.

Maintenance of Whet Stones

Keep them clean with damp shop towel.

Maintenance of P-tex Candles
Do not store near heat, as P-tex candles are made to burn and melt. Store them in a freezer to cut down on carbon build-up while burning.

Maintenance of Ski Wax
Store covered in a cool, dry place.

Maintenance of Scouring Pads
Replace when caked with debris.

Maintenance of Waxing Iron
While the iron is cool, clean the surface with a household cleaner and a paper towel.

APPENDIX B
SPECIAL CONSIDERATIONS OF SINTERED BASES

In manufacturing a sintered ski base, instead of melting base material (polyethylene) into a mold, the sintered base is formed when thousands of tiny spheres of base material are compressed into the mold and fused together with pressure and heat, but without melting and breaking down the chemical components of the base material. The result is a much harder, faster and more porous base material that is capable of soaking in more wax and withstanding more abrasion than a conventional base. Most high-performance skis now have the sintered base as a standard feature.

P-tex Application Onto a Sintered Base

One drawback to the durable sintered base is that once damage occurs, it is more difficult to repair. P-tex is more reluctant to bond to the sintered base because of its hard character. If you own a ski with a sintered base, it may be worth your while to purchase a tool called a base extruder.

The extruder works like a glue gun. It simply feeds heated—not ignited—P-tex into the gouge, while simultaneously heating the ski base. The result: a softer base for the P-tex to adhere to, a less chemically depleted bead of P-tex and a much stronger bond. This is not to say that an ignited, dripped-in bead of P-tex will not adhere to a sintered base; the difference is the quality of a longer lasting repair. Less expensive extruders that work very well can be purchased for around $100 to $150 through any ski shop.

Cleaning a Sintered Base

Since a sintered base is more porous than a conventional base, it may require greater effort to clean.

Waxing a Sintered Base

Due to the porous character of a sintered base, you should spend more time ironing wax into it, since it will take in and retain more wax than a conventional base.

APPENDIX C

SKI-NATOMY

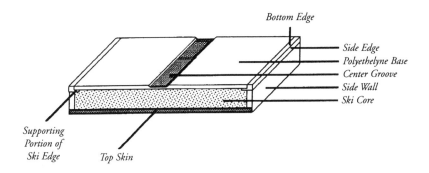

Bottom Edge
Side Edge
Polyethelyne Base
Center Groove
Side Wall
Ski Core
Supporting
Portion of
Ski Edge
Top Skin

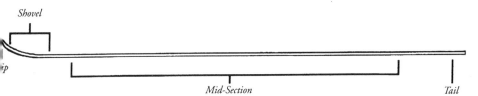

Shovel
Tip
Mid-Section
Tail

Appendix D
Summary of Tuner's Tips

1.   "WHAT'S IN A NAME?"

Always tune your skis From Tip to Tail. If a ski is tuned from the tail to the tip, tiny burrs and shavings on the base are left protruding forward. This only creates drag on the skis.

2.   "PRACTICE MAKES PERFECT CENTS."

Before you begin working on your own set of premium skis, you may want to practice a few times on an expendable set of skis that you are not afraid to damage— especially during the edge sharpening process. If you don't have a used pair of alpine skis laying around in the basement or garage, you might consider buying an old set from a ski shop, or through the classified ads. You could find this $30.00 to $40.00 investment to be a great learning tool.

3.   "GET SOME AIR."

Be certain that your work area is well-ventilated, especially when using cleaning solvents. Proper ventilation will also protect you from wax smoke when hot-waxing your skis. Both solvent fumes and wax smoke can be hazardous if breathed and can cause irritation to eyes and nasal passages.

4.   "STEEPER IS SHARPER!"

With the tip of the scraper blade filed squarely, the steeper (or closer to vertical) angle you use while scraping, the more base material the scraper will remove. If you scrape with an angle too close to horizontal, the blade will skid over the base inefficiently and remove little material.

5.   "DON'T BE DULL!"

The scraper should be kept extremely sharp at all times because a dull scraper may burnish (close pores) the base material and hinder wax penetration.

6. "COOL IS CLEAN IS COOL."

An additional way to keep carbon from building up on
ing P-tex is to store it in the freezer until you are ready to
The colder temperature reduces the rate at which carbon w

7. "FILES EVERLASTING."

As you sharpen the ski edges, alternate the areas of the file y
use. This will not only offer fresh, clean file teeth to cut with e
time, but it also will prolong the life of your file. Also rememb
clean your file with the file card after every two to three strokes.

8. "TWO IS A CROWD."

Always work on one edge at a time. This allows you to concentrate on one area, instead of trying to maintain stability and consistency on both edges at the same time.

9. "A MARKED DIFFERENCE."

You may want to mark the entire length of the edge with a felt-
tip marker. As the file runs over the marked edge, it removes the
ink and allows you to quickly determine which areas of the edge
have been sharpened and which areas require more work.

10. "SAVINGS GOES BOTH WAYS."

In order to reduce undue wear on the edge, as well as save effort
and time, you can prolong the sharpness of a beveled edge by simply sharpening only the side edge of the ski periodically.

11. "WAXED FOR ACTION!"

Ideally, skis should be waxed every one to two skiing days, as waxing is one of the most important factors to influence the overall
performance of the skis.

12. "CERTIFIABLY SAFE."

At the beginning of each ski season, have a certified binding technician inspect your boot/binding system. This should include calibration and readjustment of your bindings, if necessary, to their
proper release settings according to your weight, height, age, boot
size, and skiing style or ability.

the burn-
use it.
ill form.

ou
ach
r to